Scrapbooking Made Easy

Paper Doll Collection

Jill A. Rinner

contents

A Red Point Publishing Title

Red Point Publishing
P.O. Box 160
Pleasant Grove, UT
84062

all about paper doll art

Welcome to my paper doll collection! I hope you will have as much fun making these dolls as I did designing them. Since I began writing the "Scrapbooking Made Easy" series, I have received so many positive comments from people everywhere who are learning and finding inspiration in these booklets. (Someone told me that I even *made sense!* Now that was a compliment!) I love the excitement that I have seen in people who are thrilled about discovering new ways to bring their memories to life. This book provides you with another way to bring a personal focus to all of your wonderful scrapbook pages, greeting cards, invitations and other paper art. Paper dolls can be a way we can let a different part of our personality out to have fun!

Why paper dolls?

When I was younger, my fetish for paper exhibited itself in the form of paper dolls. I would sit for hours cutting out the dolls and playing with them, giving them funny voices and creating real-life scenarios. Today, I'm still having a blast making paper dolls (though I talk to myself less), but the reasons are even more special. These die cut paper dolls have provided another way to exhibit my own creativity and personal style in all of my paper projects, especially my scrapbook pages.

Where can I find the die cuts?

Hopefully, the retail stores near you have seen the vision and fun that comes from die cut art and have ordered these die cuts made by Accu-Cut Systems. If they haven't, then show them this book and tell them to get with it! However, if you live in a town that has not caught the scrapbooking bug (is there even such a town?), I have provided you with the basic shapes of these paper dolls in the back of this book. Use these shapes to make your own templates and create these cute paper dolls for hours of paper art fun.

They look cute, but are they easy?

Turn back and look at the cover. Do you see the word "easy"? Well then, there you go! Actually, these die cut dolls are very easy to make. In fact, you will have such a good time that we should probably change the name to "Scrapbooking Made Fun." But really, with the help of your stickers and punches (items you probably already have in your scrapbook toolbox), these paper dolls could be another great excuse not to do any housework (as if we need an excuse?).

What's the point?

Personality, of course. When scrapbooking, look inside your pictures for clues on how to dress your dolls. Bring the memory to life by dressing your paper dolls to add to the theme of your page. Remember to keep it simple though—you do not want to detract from the pictures, but merely enhance the theme you have chosen. When making cards or invitations, paper dolls can be dressed up and accessorized to match the person who is receiving the card! Match the hair color, a favorite outfit, or a hobby or sport enjoyed by the lucky recipient and so on.

What supplies do I need?

All of these things are probably currently found in your craft toolbox.

Bare Basics: scissors, chisel-tip glue pen, glue stick, black marker (thin), pencil, and ruler.

Advanced: regular hole punch, craft knife/mat, personal trimmer, color markers, and tweezers.

Highly Creative: various craft punches, unique-edge scissors, stickers, and watercolors/brush.

Don't forget to always save all of your paper scraps (organized, of course) of acid-free cardstock and pattern papers. Using these to accessorize and personalize your paper dolls is the best time to put all of those tiny pieces to use.

Where else can I find ideas on embellishing?

Children's books have the best colorful graphics for ideas on how to dress your paper dolls. Also, check out mail order clothing catalogs and your own closet for outfit ideas. But the best ideas will be found in the lives represented in your photographs that you will scrapbook. Clothing, themes and actions can be taken right from your pictures and mimicked on the paper doll that can decorate and enhance the theme of your page.

Getting Started

Die cut art has quickly become my favorite way to embellish my scrapbook pages and other paper projects. (If you are not familiar with the basics of die cut art, refer to *Designer Die Cuts* in the Scrapbooking Made Easy booklet series.) With the use of the original die cuts, you can create these paper dolls in a jiffy. However, you certainly are not limited if you do not have access to them! The various paper doll shapes located in the back of this booklet will allow you to create your own templates for the basic doll and clothing.

Embellishing your paper dolls

When embellishing your die cuts, keep these tips in mind:

- Always have the main die cut as your backdrop to build the other pieces on. In this case, it is the paper doll body.
- Die cuts have a wrong and right side. Check to make sure you have the right side showing on your finished project.
- When trimming off excess paper from embellishments you have added, turn the die cut over to the wrong side so you can see the original shape and use it as a cutting guideline.
- Do not over glue. Doing so creates smudges on your paper. This is why a glue pen is best for control.

How to Use this Book

The samples in this book are decorated but kept basic so you can see the fun and ease of creating these embellished paper dolls. Looking at the pictures, you can easily see which basic clothing shapes were used to dress the paper doll. The notes above the pictures will explain if anything different was done to create the image you are seeing. Other ideas are added to get your creative thoughts flowing! Remember to add your own personality, making the dolls look like people you know! Try different faces, experiment with cutting the doll into different positions, and don't be afraid to freehand cut unique shapes to embellish and personalize your doll. Have a paper doll fashion show that will put Paris to shame! You will soon be creating paper dolls to dazzle all of your paper projects—from bulletin boards to gift tags, memory books and beyond.

simple dot eyes
eyes & hole-punch cheeks
heart-punch cheeks
eyes, cheeks & mouth
eyes & large smile
eyes & curved smile
eyes, nose & mouth
eyes & open mouth
realistic face
eyes with color
eyes with glasses
face with freckles
faces & hair
add barrettes
add hole punch for hair ties
add headband
add stickers for bow
back of head
2-layered hairstyle
2-layered hairstyle
2-layered hairstyle
marker lines as hair strands
alter die cut for effect
trim die cut for style
hair? who needs hair?

For hands on hips or holding an item (i.e., book, bouquet, etc.), cut off a portion of the arms. Switch the left piece to the right arm and the right piece to the left arm (this enables you to maintain the right side of the die cut facing up). Create desired angle and glue. For a hands-to-mouth effect, cut off a larger portion of the arm. Switch pieces to opposite sides and glue at desired angle. For hands raised, cut off entire arm at body. Switch pieces to opposite side and glue at desired angle.

position & movement

Giving legs motion can be done a few different ways. Cut into leg where leg and torso meet. Do not cut all the way through leg, leaving a small piece intact to act as a "hinge." Repeat for clothing.

Also, legs or arms can be completely removed and reattached to clothing. For example, to make doll kneel, remove bottom of feet as shown. Switch pieces to opposite sides and glue at desired angle.

TIP: To create motion on legs and arms in more than one spot, a second paper doll can be used—cut it apart and add as an extension if the desired angle is causing the original doll appendage to appear too short.

Party Girl—cut length of jumper short for mini dress. Pearls are made with a regular hole punch.

Clown—cut large scallop collar from two beards. Use small sun punch for party hat trim. Cheeks are small circle punch.

Grad Guy—dress in class colors or classic black.

celebrations

Bride—cut arms in a holding pose. Add bouquet sticker or other embellishment for bouquet. Decorate veil with mini flower punch.

Groom—add boutonniere with stickers or punches.

Bridesmaid—use pom-pom die cut, floral sticker, or punch art for the bouquet.

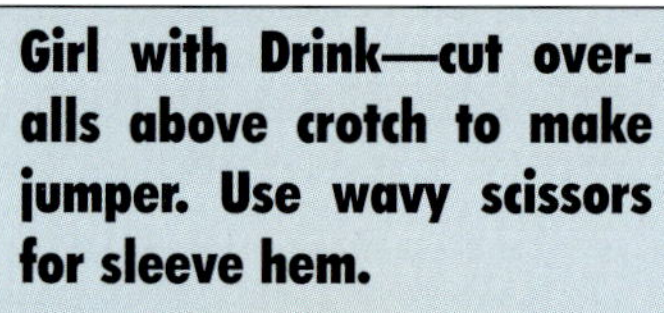

Girl with Drink—cut overalls above crotch to make jumper. Use wavy scissors for sleeve hem.

Boy with Hat—cut off excess of tank top bottom for "tucked in" look. Remove tank top and add plaid shorts under pants for boxers. Totally cool!

Sailor—add thin lines (cardstock or stickers) to vest and pants for trimming. Use a star punch or sticker on hat.

spring

These spring buddies are ready for the garden or a romp through the meadow. When cutting clothing from pattern paper, make sure you are minding the direction the pattern goes. For a no-brainer, random patterns are best. Keep it simple and refer to the clothing found in your photographs.

Girl with Bikini—cut the one piece bathing suit into a top and bottom.

Snorkeler—imagine how great this guy will look "under water"! Mask can also be used as a ski mask. Simply cut off breathing tube.

Sun Seeker—try an overview with doll lying on a towel. Stuff tote bag full of sundries needed for the beach. Add suntan lotion, pail and shovel or cover-up robe.

summer

The beach is always an interesting place to find diversity. Create dolls for various water activities: water skiing, jet skiing, sitting in an inner tube (instead of *through* it), whale watching (with binoculars), swimming (with movement of arms and legs), or diving.

Mermaid—cut off the lower body and attach mermaid tail.

Girl with Inner Tube—cut off lower body. Cut through back of inner tube and place around remaining torso.

School Girl—great for a first day of school page! Match clothing with photograph. Add a lunch bag, sports gear, gym bag, or books.

Scarecrow—add strips and hole punch to pants for suspenders. Cut "hay" with deckle-edge scissors. Cut hat on perforated line and insert head.

Yard Worker—what other fall activities do you do? Have doll carry a bushel of apples, eat a caramel apple, or sip some cider.

autumn

Sports Fan—add other gear for a tailgate party, wear a team jersey or team colors, or carry sports equipment.

Hunter—add equipment for the hunt and treasures collected from the hunt.

Fisherman—how big was the catch? Raise arm and hold a large fish or shark die cut.

Snow Friend—will yours be male or female? Make a snow friend as diverse as you.

Carolers—cut off arms and switch positions to hold caroling books.

winter

Skier—use small circle punch for earmuffs. Fitting ski pants are paper doll body in color.

Sledder—hair is behind for tucked under hat look. Ski mask is snorkel mask with breathing tube removed. Fur cuffs jazz up any jacket. To kneel, cut off legs and switch positions.

Accident victim—tight-fitting ski pants and cast are paper doll body cut in color. Headband is a 1/4" strip trimmed to match contours of head.

Volleyball Player—ponytail is piece of wavy hair design. Remove sleeves from baggy shirt. Kneepads are a 1/2" strip and small circle punch.

Basketball Player—match team colors and number of your favorite player. Remember, some of us look good with no hair. Sports equipment can be stickers or punch art.

Gymnast—for upside down look, cut off arms and ponytails and reattach to opposite side.

sports

Football Player—match team colors and number of your favorite player. Trim bike helmet by cutting out area covering the chin. Add 1" circle punch for knee pads.

Golfer—make a fashion statement with extra plaids! Hope his game is as good as he wardrobe!

Soccer Player—use 1" circle punch for knee pads. Add kicking action or bounce a ball off his head.

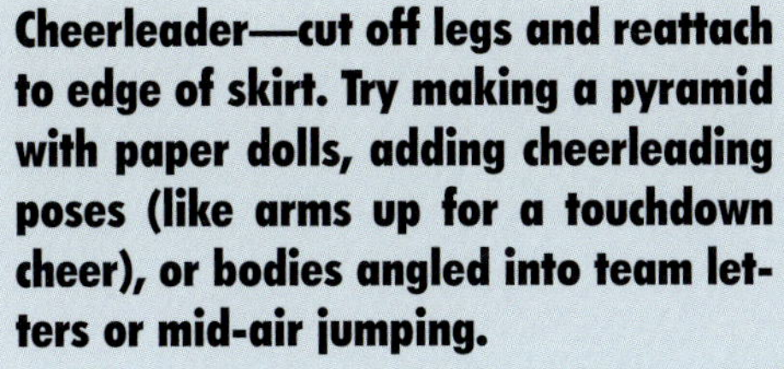

Cheerleader—cut off legs and reattach to edge of skirt. Try making a pyramid with paper dolls, adding cheerleading poses (like arms up for a touchdown cheer), or bodies angled into team letters or mid-air jumping.

In-line Skater—fitting pants are cut from paper doll body. Use regular hole punch for wheels on skates.

sports

Ice Skater—use sun punch for hat pom-pom.

Hockey Player—every good player has a few bruises! Use pink marker for scratches and scrapes. Add stick and puck die cut.

Abe Lincoln—dress in his famous attire. Make dolls for other famous Americans, such as George Washington, Martin Luther King, Jr., Betsy Ross, and others.

Leprechaun—cut hair shape in half and move pieces around head to match up with beard. To make doll shorter, trim down torso and shorten pants length.

Uncle Sam—make the same as Mr. Lincoln. You can really see the difference pattern paper makes!

holidays

Easter Girl—add bunny headband and basket with sticker eggs. Add a bonnet for a different look.

Easter Bunny—bunny suit is paper doll body with face cut out with a 1" circle punch. Add bunny headband and whiskers for full effect.

Easter Boy—pattern paper can really change the look of his outfit. Add a jacket for even dressier attire.

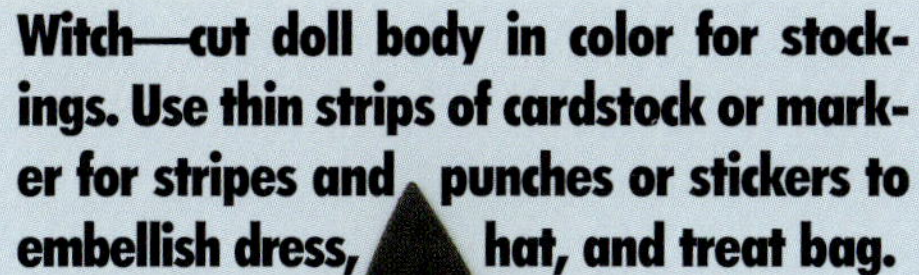

Witch—cut doll body in color for stockings. Use thin strips of cardstock or marker for stripes and punches or stickers to embellish dress, hat, and treat bag.

Vampire—cape goes behind paper doll. Bats, trickle of blood, and tombstone can "liven" things up!

Ghost—place paper doll on white cardstock and trace ghost shape freehand. Use 1/8" punch for eye holes. White opaque marker adds stitching to jeans.

holidays

Super Hero—cut paper doll body in color for form-fitting suit. Place cape behind body.

Princess—dress can be cut out of shimmery papers for a truly royal look. Add hair extensions for a Rapunzel-type character.

Apple Costume—use apple die cut. Cut slits with craft knife for arm holes. Hat is freehand. This idea can be made with any shape!

Pilgrim Man—cut collar freehand. Trim sides of hat at an angle. Cut hole in beard with knife for mouth. Shoes are cut from body shape.

Pilgrim Woman—layer back of head hair piece for bonnet. Apron is cut from a dress die cut. Can be holding pumpkin, turkey, corn or other Thanksgiving menu items.

Indian—apron is trimmed from baggy shirt. Make pouch and headband freehand.

holidays

Chinese New Year—fancy paper makes the difference with this outfit. Cut thin strips for trim and 1/8" punch for buttons.

Kwanzaa—paper for dress can be made by scanning an actual piece of cloth on a computer or color copier.

St. Lucia of Sweden—red sash has heart punches as bow. Use holly punch for wreath and make candles from thin strips of cardstock.

Santa Claus—fur accessories and black hole punch buttons dress up basic clothes for this favorite holiday visitor.

Hanukkah—Mrs. Grossman's sticker of the menorah makes this girl set for the Jewish holiday.

Angel—fancy trim is made with deckle-edge scissors. The halo is freehand.

holidays

Joseph—use a hair design for Joseph's head scarf and trim bottom edge. Embellish robe and dress with thin-colored strips.

Mary—cut arms to hold a baby. Baby Jesus wrapped in swaddling clothes is freehand.

Wise Man—stickers and opaque markers can dress up wise men and shepherds alike for their journey into Bethlehem.

France—embellish dress and hair with floral stickers. Socks are cut from doll body shape.

Zambia—warrior clothes made from skirt and winter scarf. Headress is made from beard shape. Cut fringe with scissors.

Muslim—only hands and face can show during prayer, so cover doll accordingly. Face hole made with small circle punch.

children of the world

India—changing the color cardstock you choose for the doll's body will allow you the diversity found in the human race.

Turkey—use an opaque marker to create decoration in vest. Use a hair piece for the scarf draping out of the hat.

Ethiopia—dressed for Fassika, the Easter holiday, this doll's clothes are decorated with stickers.

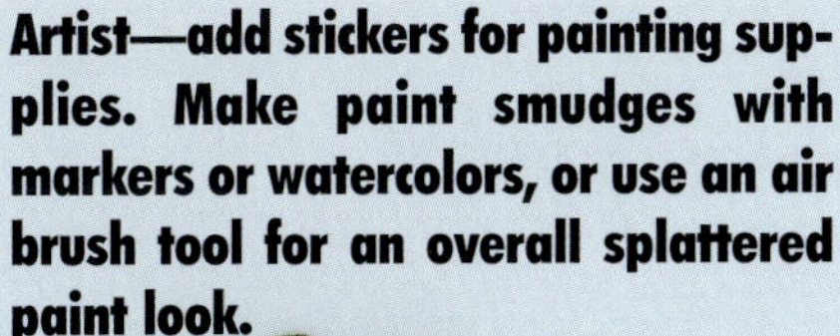

Artist—add stickers for painting supplies. Make paint smudges with markers or watercolors, or use an air brush tool for an overall splattered paint look.

Doctor—add sticker accessories or punch art as medical instruments. Add a chart, an x-ray, and a nurse helper.

Mommy—pregnant dress adds instant baby to the paper doll design. She can hold picture of an ultrasound in her hand or create an x-ray view and place it on her tummy!

occupations

Construction Worker—add whatever tools he needs to get the job done.

Baker—cut overalls above crotch level for apron. A winter mitten becomes a hot pad when cut in pattern paper. Add utensils, a BBQ, and smoke clouds for realistic effects.

Fireman—trim on jacket is made from simple strips in various sizes. Add a water hose, bucket, fire victim and dark smudges for soot.

paper doll basic shapes

These are the basic shapes that can get you started on your way to paper doll art. Embellish your paper doll shapes with the help of

- **Various punch art**
- **Additional die cut shapes**
- **Stickers**
- **Pattern and metallic papers**

To match a particular outfit in a photograph, have the actual garment material color copied or scanned via computer, and then use the custom pattern paper you have created to cut out clothing for your doll! You are only limited by your own imagination, which hopefully, is running rampant after viewing this book. May you have many playful hours of fun with your paper doll art!

about the author

Jill Rinner is a nationally recognized authority on scrapbooking. She is the author of the Scrapbooking Made Easy booklet series published by Red Point Publishing. She has taught hundreds of classes about the many facets of scrapbooking—from the basics to advanced, creative lettering and much more.

When she is not scrapbooking or writing, Jill spends time reading, traveling, organizing, and making more memories with her husband Dennis and their three children. Originally from southern California, Jill now lives in Michigan, where she is the co-owner of Our Favorite Things. Our Favorite Things specializes in scrapbook and art rubber stamp supplies with locations in Okemos and East Lansing, Michigan.

Also, Jill has a Scrapbooking Made Easy email address (SMEseries@aol.com) available for all those interested in questioning, protesting, complimenting or any comments to do with scrapbooking or her booklet series.

credits

supplies used in this book

Paper by
- Paper Patch
- Sonburn
- Frances Meyer
- Papers by Catherine
- Northern Spy

Stickers by
- Mrs. Grossman's
- Frances Meyer
- Stickopotamus
- Making Memories (alphabet and numbers)
- Melissa Neufeld
- Photo Mates

Punches by
- Marvy Uchida
- Family Treasures
- McGill

Pens by
- Marvy Uchida
- EK Success
- Sakura

Scissors and Trimmers by
- Fiskars

special thanks to

Jim, CJ, and everyone at Accu-Cut for sharing in the vision.
Thanks to my support team at home—Denny, Joe, Lizzy, and Lexy.
And to Leslie at OFT (Thanks a bunch, Lester!).
And, as always, a big huge thanks to everyone at Red Point Publishing, especially my buddy, Jeff. You rock!